THIN

THRIVE:

FITTON PRESS

Think and Thrive: How to Find Power, Happiness and
Success at Work – Without Quitting Your Job

Editor: Spencer Borup
Cover and Interior Design: Jason Anscomb

Published in Singapore by Fitton Press

ISBN: 978-981-11-6079-0

This book is dedicated to my wife, Diana, without whom
I wouldn't be the person I am today.

THINK & THRIVE:

HOW TO FIND POWER, HAPPINESS AND SUCCESS AT WORK – WITHOUT QUITTING YOUR JOB

JAMES IRVINE

CONTENTS

INTRODUCTION

For most of us, the workplace is a tough environment in which to thrive.

We work long hours in an attempt to meet our deadlines and demonstrate our commitment. We try to keep our self-respect intact as we deal with bosses, colleagues and clients in a never-ending game of one-upmanship. We even work out in the gym whenever we have a "free" moment in an effort to maintain our personal branding.

And at the end of the day (or night), we arrive home exhausted, blaming it on our dedication to the organization, when the truth is, it comes from frustration and not a little anger. In this state of exhaustion, how are we ever going to feel like doing the work we need to do to find out how to fulfil our potential?

Our potential is there inside us, waiting to be unleashed. But after fifteen years of dedication and commitment, we still feel that we have not given ourselves a chance, not found the key that unlocks the door to our happiness and success. Even though we are good at our job, we seem to be on the same treadmill we started on years ago. And so, our motivation starts to wane just a bit, and our daydreaming takes us to the beaches of Bali. We are in danger of losing our focus and letting our grip on our performance slip.

STOP. Rewind.

For you, the workplace is the perfect environment in which to thrive.

You determine how you use your day to get the job done so that you maintain a healthy work-life balance. *You* determine how you feel about yourself and use this strength to shine in the team meeting. *You* determine how you feel about someone else and who they are to you so that they can never push you around. *You* determine how you will respond to an event so that you overcome any and all challenges. *You* determine your state of mind and emotion at any time so that you are always primed to come out on top.

Which reality would you prefer?

It's entirely up to you. Your career starts and finishes with you. When you are fully in control of how you think, and therefore how you feel and act, your colleagues, your organization, your destiny and your happiness will take care of themselves.

Stop running harder and harder trying to control the world, and take control of the only thing you ever really have control of: yourself. Stop trying to influence others to do what you want. Stop trying to get on top of your work by putting in more effort. Stop trying to win more business by pushing harder on the marketplace. Stop trying to fulfil your potential by pressing harder on the world outside of yourself.

Instead, turn inward and get to know yourself; you will find that your power, happiness and success are already inside you, waiting for you to unleash them.

It all starts with how you think. This book will show you the process for becoming aware of, and then controlling, the thinking that drives your career and future destiny. Instead of just telling you to change your thinking, together we will delve into the nature of thought, how it affects every outcome you get and how you can stop it running your life without you having any control over it.

You will then learn the exact method for harnessing the power of your own thoughts to propel you forward in whatever direction you choose. You will feel the power that comes from controlling how you perceive the world minute by minute, and you will give yourself the courage to speak your truth and take actions that are in your own best interest.

I started my career like everyone else, thinking that I had to talk more loudly if I wanted to be heard, and push harder if I wanted to be effective. I thought that the nature of the game was to control my situation, my environment; and when I had control of the world, I would get whatever I wanted. I tried to get this control by working long hours and behaving more assertively, while all along my out-of-awareness thinking was making sure I didn't get it.

When I didn't get the results I fought so hard to get, I started learning about personal development, and in the process became a Master Practitioner of Neuro-Linguistic Programming (NLP). NLP taught me that what happens *inside* of us absolutely controls what happens to us in the world *outside*. And this was the key to unlock my self-respect, self-drive and progress.

When you master your own thinking, you master your emotions, speech and behavior; it is only a mastery over yourself that will yield any results. The way you perceive the world in your mind actually creates the world you end up living. You are responsible for everything that happens to you, through what you allow to happen in your mind. This is real power: the ability to exercise mastery over yourself and, hence, your world.

Once you have mastery over yourself, you can stop trying to control your destiny and allow it to unfold naturally, exactly as you wish. No more frustration. No more feeling lost. No more feeling that you have not given yourself a chance. No more feeling that you will never tap into your true potential. You will feel the power that comes from knowing that everything that happens to you is not only up to you, but within your ability to manage.

This is the true source of happiness and success at work.

Wouldn't you like to get up in the morning and look forward to the day? Wondering: *What can I excel at? What kinds of problems can I overcome? What exciting challenges lie ahead?*

Louise Hay did. Her early years were marked by a tormented upbringing of instability, impoverishment and abuse that led her to run away from home. In later life, however, she founded the successful publishing company Hay House Inc. and wrote many books, including *You Can Heal Your Life*, which became a *New York Times* Best Seller for thirteen consecutive weeks and sold over fifty million copies. In her own words:

"I changed my life when I changed my thinking."

I don't promise that this book will make you rich, but I do promise that if you incorporate the time-tested concepts in these pages, your life will change for the better.

Let me show you how to look inside yourself and work from the inside-out. Let me show you how to change your thinking and thus change your behavior for more positive results. Let me show you how to come home to your true self.

Plato said it best:

"Thinking: the talking of the soul with itself."

If you're ready, turn inside.

CHAPTER 1

THE WORLD FROM THE INSIDE-OUT

In this chapter I'm going to introduce you to a whole new way of looking at yourself, other people, and the world around you. You will learn how to find the kind of personal power and control that we all crave; how to turn your world on its head and make it work for you and never again against you. Let's get started.

Most of us try to change our life by changing the world we see Out There. By Out There, I mean anything we can see and touch: our behavior, our job, our employer, our industry, or even our country. We try to improve our confidence and self-esteem by acting more assertive. We try to improve our performance by working longer hours, working faster, or being more effective. We try to improve our happiness by changing jobs, getting into a new career, or moving to a new country.

And all this stuff that we do Out There, the improvements we try to make to our behavior, to our situation and even to our bodies is hard work. We feel that we are in a constant struggle to keep the momentum going, to stay in charge of our destiny, to just keep our head above water. We go through our careers with the mindset that we have to push, to force our way forward, to act aggressively upon the world if we are going to keep up. It's all about acting, action, taking *"massive action"* as Tony Robbins likes to say, to move forward, make progress, move on up and achieve our dreams.

And, of course, we have successes and failures, and when we succeed we feel on top of the world, for a while, until the next failure comes along, and then we feel down, disheartened, depressed. And as we ride this roller coaster of "progress" trying to improve our lives, we often feel exhausted and unfulfilled. Sometimes we ask ourselves, *"Am I ever going to get on top of this, to feel strong and powerful and successful?"*

Everyone around us, the boss and the gurus, keep telling us to be just that little bit more aggressive, prepare harder, focus more, and do the deal. Therefore we try even harder, work our butts off, and try to assert ourselves till we are emotionally worn out. It really feels as if we are on a permanent treadmill going nowhere.

This is the nature of the world perceived and lived from the outside-in. The world Out There is big and complex, however, and it doesn't make sense that one solitary person can somehow get control of it and make it bend to his or her will. It seems like an impossible dream. Wouldn't it be better if we focused on what we, as one single person, *can* control: our mind? And we are built in such a way that when we control our mind, we also control how we feel and how we act. With our thinking, our emotions and our behavior under our control, the world Out There will respond perfectly to give us what we want. This is living from the inside-out.

No more trying to control what our boss decides or how our client feels. No more trying to control whether our colleagues like us or not, or what the stock market thinks of our company. Just pay attention to *yourself:* to your thoughts, feelings and actions, and let whatever is Out There respond accordingly.

The truth is, the world Out There that we are so desperate to be in charge of doesn't actually exist. There's no such thing as an objective reality Out There that everybody subscribes to. The world is not a fact. People are not what we see or what they seem; your organization isn't a tangible entity, a fact.

Your performance at work is not an objective fact. Nor, for that matter, is your personality or are your personal qualities. They may be written on your resume, but that's all they are: bits of ink on a piece of paper or light on a screen. Even the way you are in the world, your outward behavior, isn't fixed or a fact about who you are. In effect, you're trying to gain control over something that isn't even real. No wonder we are all so exhausted.

Let me explain. The world Out There is your own creation. It's yours. It belongs to you and nobody else. And it's entirely different from the world that your colleague at the workstation near to you owns. This is because the only world we are ever able to be aware of is in our head. Yes, our eyes can see our boss talking over there, and our ears can hear her words. But when our eyes and ears take in the light and sounds emanating from our boss, we don't photocopy her in our mind. We don't re-produce "her" inside our mind, as if she were a product on a factory line being reproduced in the exact same way in thousands of people's minds.

Instead, we re-present her in our mind; we take in the sensory signals and present her to ourselves again, in a different format, in our mind. We interpret her in our own way. She may talk in an abrupt, aggressive way or in a gentle, caring way, but those words, "abrupt," "aggressive," "gentle," "caring," are not facts. They are our personal interpretations. We create them as we think about her as she is speaking to us.

You may say, "Everyone knows what abrupt is, so that must be what she is," but that assumption is also just yours, and is in no way a common judgment about the world. One of your colleagues may find her short, sharp diction entirely satisfying and helpful because he values that kind of communication. He might call her "professional" instead of "abrupt." On the other hand, many people may find what you deem to be "gentle" and "caring" to be slow, weak and annoying.

In sum, the world Out There is actually only inside our mind. Our boss in front of us is just a neutral bundle of flesh and bone. Even her communication is neutral. That is, until we get hold of all of that and put our own, individual judgment on it.

In fact, our mind is so powerful that when we go away we may well remember her physical attributes as different from what we saw when she was in front of us. And don't forget, when we come to describing her physical attributes to someone else, we will apply our *own* ideas about her, whether she is "skinny" or "overweight" or whatever. None of it is fact; it is all subjective.

And that subjective perception is our reality. It is real to us. It is actually the world we live in.

Let's go a bit deeper into how we interpret her in our own mind. The key word here is "re-present." We present her again in our mind. We take the person we see in front of us, and place her on a kind of movie screen in the back of our mind and "see" and "hear" her again. Stop now and think of your boss. Can you "see" him or her? Where is he or she? What is he or she doing? Can you "hear" this person? What is he or she saying?

Your boss is nowhere in sight, but I bet you can run a vivid movie of him or her in your mind. And I'm sure that it's so vivid that it gives you pretty strong feelings. But nothing is going on Out There. You may be sitting in an armchair at home, yet a very realistic set of images and sounds is flashing through your mind.

That's what we do when we think. We use the same senses internally as we use in the world outside to see, hear, taste, touch and smell.

Try this: think about a lemon. Look at it. Pick it up and feel it to the touch. Now get a knife and cut it in half. Now lean your head back and open your mouth and squeeze the juice from the lemon into your mouth. Wow! Can you taste it? Did it make you wince involuntarily? Wasn't that short movie fun? You can try this experiment anytime you like to get away from what's in front of you. Fancy a holiday in Bali? Run a movie seeing through your own eyes as you lie on your stomach being massaged on the beach while looking up at ... well, you know.

But that's only the beginning of the story. When we run a movie of our boss in our mind, we create a complete character, not just a picture and a soundtrack. We see her facial expressions as she's talking Out There and then we re-present them in our own way; we interpret them, give our own personal meaning to them. Similarly, when we hear her words and tone Out There, we re-present these and give them our own spin. And as we do this time after time, we build up a complex character, the person we call our boss. And she is very real to us.

And so she becomes our personal creation with very little, or perhaps even nothing, to do with who she thinks she is and who anybody else thinks she is. She, as a person, is not real. There is no objective, factual, real person out there, because she can only ever live in somebody's mind as their representation, their interpretation, of what their senses pick up Out There.

"Reality" doesn't exist. Yes, you can say to me, "Look at that beautiful tree over there. Don't tell me it doesn't exist, that it's not real," and it certainly does seem to be a definite fact. But if you want to take it to an extreme, I might say that the colors you see and the substance you touch still reside in your mind. Your senses of sight and touch represent the impulses they receive in your mind, and that is what you label a tree. What it really is or isn't we will never truly know. A quantum physicist may even tell you that it's just energy, or that it doesn't actually exist until you become conscious of it. But that's not for me to explain!

Even though there is no objective reality Out There, there certainly is a very real one In Here, in your mind. If you stop and turn inward for a moment, become aware of your thoughts right now, you will realize that you are creating them yourself; they are not fed to you or put upon you by anyone else.

Somebody you are having a conversation with may say or do something that annoys you, but the thought that causes you to get annoyed is your own creation. It is your choice. You could have looked at that person and listened to his words and had an entirely different thought, which would have caused you have an entirely different emotion. You didn't *have* to get annoyed. It wasn't inevitable, written in your stars.

When you think about it, the world you live in is all just your thoughts, your awareness, your mind functioning beautifully. Everything: every person, the kind of organization you work for, the nature of your job, all of it is subject to interpretation by you, is real only insofar as you are aware of it. And that reality is all your own doing.

What does this mean? If the world resides in your mind, then it is no longer the immovable giant Out There that you are spending so much energy trying to control, to influence, to move out of your way. In fact, it is the most movable, pliable, changeable thing in your life. You actually own it, and **it can change just as easily and quickly as you can change your mind.**

It means that we no longer have to make our boss an ogre, a monster, a person to be feared, if we do not wish to. It's entirely up to us. And that's the true source of our power. We can choose to create any world we like inside our minds such that it becomes our reality.

Let's say you think your boss is a bully. The person that resides in your mind is someone who is not nice and caring, but nasty and cold. This movie that you have of him will cause you to have certain feelings, such as anger, resentment, and fear.

With these feelings inside you, you will act in certain ways when you come face to face with him. You may be passive aggressive and make angry faces and refuse to contribute information. This behavior will be picked up by your boss and interpreted in *his* own way. He may conclude that you are an uncooperative team member. And that, his conclusion about you, will have further repercussions on how he treats you.

On the other hand, you can come into the office one day and decide, for your own benefit, that your boss is actually a pussycat and acts tough and bullying to cover up his true nature. With that one change of thought, of character in your internal movie, everything else changes. You feel more confident and less antagonistic toward him. Your communication then changes as you negotiate with him from a stronger standpoint.

That has further repercussions on how he interprets *you* in his mind and behaves toward you. This creates new kinds of results for you. In fact, this one change in your reality can have many wide ramifications extending a long way down the road.

At the end of the day, it all originates in your own thinking about your boss, the reality of the person he is in your mind. In other words, the way you think creates your own idea of what is real, and also causes actual things to happen in your life, whether you wanted them or not. You think that your boss treating you, as you see it, unfairly is something you have no control over; that it comes from his personality and who he is. The reality is that you are "at cause" in every result you get, whether you are aware of it or intend it or not.

And this is the true meaning of responsibility, the fact that the world Out There is not responsible for anything that happens to us, but responds perfectly to whatever reality we create in our minds through our thinking. We have "ultimate power" as Tony Robbins once told us. We are the pure creators of our own reality, our own life, and our own results. We are not the hapless victims of whatever the world chooses to throw at us. We are not powerless, helpless, or stuck.

But I haven't told you the whole story. The truth is, we are only fully in control if we are *aware* of what we are doing with our mind from moment to moment and consciously manage our thinking in the way we want to. But nearly all of us, except the occasional mystic in Nepal, are actually controlled by an unseen force that goes right back to our beginning. This is our programming, our "domestication" as Don Miguel Ruiz calls it in his revelatory book *The Four Agreements*.

And this programming, as the word suggests, runs

in the back of our mind and controls just about every interaction, decision, self-concept and so on that we have. If we feel that we have little self-esteem and are scared to stand up to people whom we perceive as being more powerful than us, you can be sure the source of this mindset is our programming. And we are not even aware of it.

Let's go back to our example of our bullying boss to explain. Let's say he comes to you and says, "Get me the report by tomorrow, first thing," and you react instantly with the thought, "He's pushing me too hard, I don't have enough time. And anyway, I don't like the way he said it. He didn't ask me, he ordered me." That's entirely your own interpretation of what and how your boss communicated.

But as you go back to your workspace you think some more, "People shouldn't order other people around. That's not fair; that's bullying." Now, this thought isn't a direct reaction to the conversation you just had with your boss. It's another thought about your first reaction, your first thought. It's not your immediate interpretation of what transpired between you and your boss Out There in the world, but rather, it's an additional construction of your own mind.

You thought about the thought that he "ordered you," and came up with the conclusion that he had bullied you. You have created a reality right out of your own mind, not as a result of anything Out There in the world. You have interpreted your previous interpretation, and come up with the label "bully" for your boss, which is a pure fabrication even though it appears to be real to you.

But it doesn't necessarily stop there. You can continue thinking about those thoughts. You can tell yourself, "All people who tell others what to do without asking or consulting them are bullies." Once again you have had a thought about the previous thought that your boss bullied you. You have climbed even further up and away from the world Out There, moved into the world of pure concepts, pure imagination, and now created a *belief* about people.

That's what we do. We don't just react once to something that goes on Out There in the world. We think about that outside event, and then think about *that* thought. Instead of just thinking that you didn't like the abrupt way your boss ordered you around, you now think about that and conclude that he is a bully. Now we have left the outside event and started to think about it in a more conceptual way. And when we take that thought one step further and think that all people who speak abruptly are bullies, we have climbed higher and further away from the original event and entered the world of ideas.

This is where our beliefs and assumptions about the world we live in reside. We have the ability to create an entire world out of thin air, one that doesn't have much to do with the world Out There at all. If we're not careful, we can end up totally divorced from reality. (I'm using the word "reality" here to mean the world we can see, hear, touch etc.) Then we are labelled insane.

Going back to your belief about your boss being a bully, you are now able to take this belief and spread it beyond your interaction with your boss. You can now apply it to anyone who dares to speak to you in an abrupt way (in your interpretation). You have moved way beyond the simple one-off interaction with your boss. And as you move this belief around, finding more and more "bullies" out there, more and more examples to confirm your belief, the belief entrenches itself and gets fixed in your mind as a part of your everyday thinking, your actual reality. It's as if you have written your own program for your mind.

We call this kind of pattern of thought a "Frame of Reference," because it acts as a frame for all the assumptions and conclusions we make about people based on this one thought. With the frame that "people who tell others what to do without asking or consulting them are bullies," we tend to respond to such behavior in a negative way, for example with anger or resentment. And with a feeling of anger or resentment, we will tend to behave in a way that may damage the relationship, with all the consequences that that may bring. Thus we can see how a pattern of thought that we ourselves create in our mind can lead to real world results.

How many frames do you think you have that are running your work life and level of success, without you ever being aware of them? Frames could be beliefs, understandings, decisions, conclusions, whatever thoughts we have that recur over and over again and direct our moment by moment interpretations of people and events, as well as our feelings about them and our behavioral responses.

This is our programming, and much of it comes from our early days, conclusions we make about the world as we are growing up in our families, and learnings we gather as we experience friendships, educators, and people who give us pain or pleasure. This programming is a series of frames that are outside our conscious awareness but that absolutely control our every action and reaction and the kind of life we lead.

We are controlled by our inner "stuff," our internal world, which we project out onto the external world and create either our own heaven or our own hell. No wonder we often say to ourselves, "What went wrong? Why didn't I make it while she made it?" We ascribe all kinds of reasons for feeling less than others, to things out there like competitive colleagues, an unappreciative boss, a lousy company, the wrong job, a bad marriage, and so on and so on. We do this when all along we have been at cause; we have been the creator of our reality, through our internal stuff, our moment-by-moment thinking and our frames. If you want to go deeper into the idea of frames and how they drive your life, I owe a debt of gratitude to L. Michael Hall and his life-changing book *The Secrets of Personal Mastery.*

Where do we go from here? Well, you don't have to accept that you have no control. While it's true that the way our career turns out is determined in large part by our programming, our frames, it's not true that we have no control over it.

The secret is to STOP. Stop chasing shadows out there in the world. Stop giving yourself pressure and stress trying to force yourself to act differently. Stop writing down hard goals and then chasing after them with willpower and effort. Stop changing job, company, industry, city or country in an effort to find your fit in the world of work. Stop running your present responsibilities down because you don't feel sufficiently passionate about them. And stop comparing yourself unfavorably to those who you think have made it in their careers, labelling yourself as lost or worse, a loser.

Instead, START turning inward. Forget about what's going on Out There for a while. Rather, notice how you are feeling right now. Really become aware of it, notice where it is in your body, how strong it is, and whether it is new or has been recurring a lot recently. Give it a word to identify it. Are you fully aware of how you are feeling? Good.

Now, go back one step and identify what you were thinking that led to that feeling. It didn't just appear. Something that was going on in your mind led to it. Can you see it? Can you see your internal movie, the pictures and sounds that make up your thought? Can you see the people, the place, the colors, the movement, hear the voices and noises? Give yourself a while to fully experience your internal movie, your thought.

Now you are in control. Once you can become aware of what is going on in your mind—the source of all your results—then you have the power to do something with it.

Showing you what to do and how to take back control of your career and your destiny is my mission for the rest of this book. So turn the page and we will start this journey by showing how you can think about your Self differently, the person who is going to move forward with a strength and power you have only dreamed about.

CHAPTER 2

A NEW

IDENTITY

Who am I? What is my identity? These two questions have ignited in us a search for our true place in the world of work, and often lead nowhere or send us in the wrong direction. The result has often been deep frustration, dissatisfaction, and the sense that we are somehow lost. In this chapter I offer you a completely new way to think about yourself, one that gives you freedom and personal power and results that are right for *you*. But first, let's talk a bit about where I went wrong.

I thought I knew who I was. My father was a businessman, and I saw this hero who had our family name in the company name and who seemed to run the show his way. He wasn't like all those other fathers who had to answer to bosses. I used to follow him to the factory on Saturday mornings and marvel as he solved problems with his staff and made crucial decisions. I even worked in the factory when I was on holiday from university, so I became fairly familiar with the business. Little did I know how these experiences growing up would create ideas about myself in my mind, would create a frame that would control a future decision about my career. A decision that, looking back, may not have been in my best interests.

No, I didn't join the family company and follow in my father's footsteps. My father passed away before I finished university, and my instinct led me to search for a job that took me overseas. I had studied and loved economics, and so I leaned toward a job in an international bank. And when the interview went well, I joined them on the overseas management trainee program.

Before I set off for my new job, I popped into my father's old office, which was now occupied by a new managing director. My father's old secretary, whom I had known since I was young, was still working there. When I told her that I was going to become a banker she jumped in her seat, shocked, and said, "You, a banker? I can't believe it!" She wasn't congratulating me on getting a hard-to-win job. She was telling me that she didn't think I was at all suited to the role or image of a banker. And she should know!

That one, highly charged remark, combined with an already embedded idea about myself as more of a businessman like my father, implanted a frame in my mind that said, **"You're not really a banker. You're**

too dynamic to really be a banker." Despite this, I went ahead with my plan to work in an international bank because I had a strong desire to live and work overseas, and was prepared to do any job that accomplished this for me. But the seeds of doubt and disruption had been planted.

Fast forward six years and I'm sitting in my office in the bank in Brunei, South East Asia. In comes one of my customers, a successful insurance salesman, and I start thinking, "If only I was doing what he is doing, going out every day and meeting clients and marketing himself and running his own show." Later, in comes the country manager of a security company, and then afterward the country manager of a major airline, and once again I'm thinking, "These people really run the show, they make their own decisions, and they have none of the constrictions I face as a banker. I can't even get out of the office when I want to. If only I had the freedom they have!"

In this way, I spend my time dreaming about the day I finally have my "freedom," the day I'm a marketing man, a businessman, anything but a banker. The result? I'm not focused on my moment-by-moment work, not motivated to improve my knowledge or skills as a banker. I have already quit in my mind, so what's the point of doing my best, concentrating and working assiduously if I'm going to leave at the end of the day anyway?

You see, this frame that I'm actually a dynamic, outgoing, marketing or businessman type, this ideal Self that I had constructed, was directly controlling my destiny. I thought the bank was too old-fashioned, didn't care about its staff, and wasn't the kind of place I should be working in. And of course, it was and wasn't any of those things. It just was.

The reality of the bank merely lived in my head, and that of anyone else who worked there. And that reality was different in the heads of each and every one of my colleagues. It was a different bank to everyone. Its identity and nature was thus limitless. But because I carried around this ideal Self in my mind, this frame that I was actually somebody not suited to a job in a bank, I then couldn't find any redeeming factors in either my job, my career or my employer. I had to leave.

And so the frame of my ideal Self, controlled my outcome. I quit my job as a banker and entered a career counselling program to help me find out what I was best suited for. But my ideal Self followed me there, and so I answered a Myers-Briggs type personality questionnaire according to who I *thought* I was, this Self that I had constructed and turned into some kind of holy grail. The report identified me as an extrovert, uncomfortable with the kind of work needed in a bank. What's new? I didn't need to spend a lot of money on career counselling to discover that.

Except that it was all wrong. What seemed obvious to me at the time, that I wasn't suited to being a banker because I was more outgoing and dynamic, was a load of nonsense. It was all false. What I now know, much to my delight I might add, is that I am very much an introvert and find the company of people for any extended period of time positively draining. I get really energized when I am alone, reading a good book or delving into stuff inside my mind. And the fairly quiet, concentrated paperwork needed in my old role in the bank, I now realize, would have suited me just fine if I had had the right mindset, if I had not been controlled by this powerful frame that I was anything but a banker at heart.

The lesson, of course, is "Know thyself." Look to your past actions and preferences and identify what kind of personality you have. When I looked back much later I noticed that I always loved spending time on my own, doing cross-country running or reading or listening to music (always with headphones on, sealed off from the rest of the people in the room). I spent my secondary school and university days in the library, in silence, where I could study and enjoy all the realizations and understandings that were coming to me. At work, even though I was among people most of the time, I would always have my lunch alone, just to recharge my batteries. And I just loved concentrating on something challenging that was right in front of me, not Out There among other people.

The problem is that there are so many influences Out There in the world, competing for our attention so that they can motivate us to be like any highly successful go-getter with a high profile and tons of respect and adulation. We are given "traits of winners" and think that to be a winner ourselves we have to have these traits. And so we create this person that we wish we could be in our mind, this fictitious personality with all the qualities the outside tells us are admirable and worthy of respect.

It's difficult to try to be someone we're not, so we think we are less than this ideal person. We work out harder, work at our desks harder, and search for any opportunity to become the person we have set up in our mind. We quit our job because we think that it is not enough for us, that there are better opportunities out there. We read books and attend seminars about personal branding, starting your own business, and getting the client. And somewhere in a prominent place in all the books and seminars is a section on how to create the identity for success, how to become a certain kind of person, a go-getter, a great salesperson, a great presenter. And surprise, surprise, the kind of person every guru tells us to be is more or less the same: an outgoing, marketing, businessperson type of person, who simply has to be good at public speaking.

What's really going on here? Well, let's go back a bit. We have already established that there is no such thing as a real world. That the world out there that we think is a fact is actually a very personal, individual creation that we have made inside our own minds.

The people we interact with on a moment-by-moment basis are not really the office bully or the sensitive one but are just neutral, waiting for us to ascribe traits and personalities to them based on our age-old inner stuff reaching out and touching them like some kind of magic wand. In fact, they are just getting on with their lives in the best way they know how.

But we are far from neutral. We listen to them and watch them and re-present them in our minds in our own way, turning them into either a Dr. Jekyll or a Mr. Hyde. We *give* them an identity, they don't send their identity to us. In the minds of a thousand, different people, the person working next to you might have a thousand different identities.

The truth is, you may be a different person, have a different identity, in the minds of each one of your colleagues. There's no way you can control this. You can't create an ideal identity out of your books and seminars and insert it into the minds of other people. They will read you as they wish, based not just on how you present yourself to the world, but mainly on their own inner stuff projecting outwards onto you. And they will see their projection of you, not the flesh and bones person standing in front of them.

So forget about being your ideal Self. Stop trying to be somebody you're not. Not only will this possibly drive you in the wrong direction in your career and motivate you to make decisions that harm you, but also you will never be the person you want to be anyway, because you live in the minds of other people. They will create you, and you will never really know who you are to them.

If we are all just a creation of our and other people's minds, then who we are is immaterial. We are nothing. We are not real. Yes, we are flesh and bone and brain, but even the quantum theorists will assert that at the end of the day we are just energy. Even your behavior, your culture, your qualifications and your job are not who you are. They also live in the mind, are subjective interpretations, movies in the mind, both yours and others'. How you behave, how you speak, for example, doesn't tell anyone who you are, because you (hopefully) speak differently to different people based on the person and situation.

Which speech is the real you? You probably have multiple different ways of speaking to someone, and since this changes moment by moment there's no way anyone can create an identity of you around that. It's the same with expressing your emotions. You may be an angry tyrant in one situation and a quiet lamb in another, depending entirely on the circumstances, the context.

What about our self-concept, who we are to ourselves? We can't really say who we are with any definiteness. And when we insist on defining ourselves as an MBA-qualified banker or an ex-SAS motivational speaker, we put ourselves in a straightjacket and narrow our vision of our destiny. Not only that, we put enormous pressure on ourselves to live up to our so-called identity.

The next time you attend a cocktail party and somebody says, "So, what do you do?" you might as well say, "I just am," because you really don't have an identity, and you really are just a bit of breeze, or energy, or spirit if you prefer.

But this is where the fun starts. If you don't have a fixed identity, if you really are not your upbringing, your culture, your nationality, your qualifications or your job, then you are free to create anybody you like for yourself. Yes, of course you are working in a specific job with certain important skills, but you are not defined by these and you are free to be whoever you want from one moment to the next. You are not tied down to being a certain way just because in the past you have identified yourself as such.

You are now as free to be as assertive, or might I say aggressive, as you wish if you have been a wallflower up to now. You are free to say what you really want to say, to stand up and challenge people in one situation, and then decide to keep your own counsel in another. You are not stuck the way you are today. In fact, you can start each day with a clean slate if you wish. Nobody out there can tell you who you are or expect you to be anybody other than exactly who you wish to be at any moment.

And since you are just energy, or spirit, you can read each situation moment to moment and flex yourself accordingly: adapt and respond to each situation in exactly the right way to achieve your purpose. You don't have to be a tyrant in every situation just because in your mind you have always believed you have to be strong and pushy. You don't have to be the helpful one every time just because that's who you have always thought of yourself as, identified yourself as. And you don't have to be scared, hesitant or nervous among people just because that's who you always thought of yourself as. Move around like a wisp of smoke, changing shape as you meet one obstacle after another.

Easier said than done, right? The key to changing who you are and becoming more flexible and adaptable is to change the way you think about yourself. You can think about yourself as a wisp of smoke, a powerful person, a strategist, a supremely confident person, or whatever frame gives you the impetus to change the way you usually behave. I like the "wisp of smoke" frame, because it gives me the power to be tactical and flexible when I deal with people. I can read the situation and decide what kind of behavior best suits my purpose and best responds to the other person to achieve what I want.

And as a wisp of smoke I can stand back from getting too involved and personal, and focus on my objective.

In addition to using the frame "wisp of smoke," I also use the frame "I'm just OK as I am right here and now." This, to me, is my take on the concept of self-acceptance.

When we simply accept ourselves just as we are, we give ourselves permission to just be sitting where we are, doing what we are doing, thinking what we are thinking, and saying what we are saying, and feel fine and comfortable, and incredibly powerful. No guilt. No thoughts that we should be doing what somebody else expects us to do in their mind. No thinking that we have left something undone. No feelings that we have done something wrong, or that we are in some way bad, or that we have somehow displeased someone. No thinking that anyone is upset with us, disappointed in us, or angry at us. We just are, and that's OK.

That's because it's all generated by us, not by anybody else. The pressure, the stress, all those anxious thoughts are our own personal creation, and they belong entirely and exclusively to us. They are ours alone. Nobody else's. We own it and that's all there is. Once we accept that anxious thoughts are created just by us and not by the way somebody else behaves, then we can relax and accept that fact and be OK with it. The secret is that once we accept ourselves as owning our anxious thoughts and being OK with it, the anxiety tends to go away. We then feel calm and happy with ourselves. And nobody, but nobody, has the right to invade this ownership, to invade our idea of ourselves as perfectly OK just as we are.

This idea, this concept called self-acceptance, once

again, is a frame. It is a conceptual thought that puts a frame around, and sets up, many other thoughts that we use to deal with our everyday challenges and interactions. And it's amazingly powerful. When we have self-acceptance, we have the confidence to say exactly what is on our mind, to speak our truth. We know it is OK, and we don't worry about how anybody is going to react to what we say. We allow them to, and that's OK. Then we deal with that reaction in the way we want to. Nobody can make us feel small or bad.

And this idea that you have absolute control over your thinking, your frames, is the source of all your personal power. It doesn't come from outside, from somebody or some title conferring power upon you. It simply comes from knowing that you and you alone are in charge of your mind, which is the creator of how you see your Self, your colleagues and clients, your job, your organization, your capabilities and your future. All of it is within your own control. And when you have control, then you can decide what to do to achieve your full potential. It doesn't depend on anybody else deciding or doing anything. You can change your destiny simply with a change in your thinking. Everything else flows from that. It's up to you.

The frames and movies you create are personal to you. I have told you about my frame of self-acceptance and how it helps me. But you are free to build your own portfolio of frames that suit your temperament and needs, and to insert within them the movies that best help you move forward and deal with your challenges moment-by-moment. And as you gradually move forward, making things happen according to your plan, your potential will arise and your destiny will unfold.

But I'm not finished, am I? I can hear you asking, "How do I actually go about changing my frames and movies? It's all very well taking control of your reality, but how do I accomplish it?" Turn to the next chapter, and I will show you how to banish frames that are no good for you and put in your mind frames that lift you up and give you power.

CHAPTER 3

A PERFORMANCE

REVIEW

We think that performance is all about taking action that leads to tangible, measurable results. Consequently we go at it like a bat out of hell, rushing to make things happen and show our team mates how effective we are. But I want to hold you back a moment and talk first about another kind of performance: the one we absolutely must be a star at; the one we do all on our own inside ourselves. Once again, I would like to start by teaching you a hard-won lesson from my own experience.

I had it all wrong. I thought that if I was in the right job for me, my performance would soar, and if I was in the wrong job, my performance would naturally suffer. Thus began my search for the perfect job, the perfect organization, the perfect industry, the perfect country, and even the perfect business to start. Each time I was sure I would find my fit, my true place in the world, where my natural talents would shine and I would finally be successful. And each time my performance wasn't as great as I had anticipated.

Each time I decided that I hadn't quite found what I was looking for, and so my focus was back on the future, dreaming of the day I would "come home" to my true self and show the world what I was made of. I didn't concentrate on what was right in front of me, moment by moment, hour by hour. I was too distracted. I was working on a superficial plane that didn't touch the hard ground where solid reports were executed, difficult interpersonal situations were dealt with, and more business was won. I was glossing over the hard grind. The clear result: I didn't perform at any level that would raise me up in the ranks or grow my business.

You see, we're told that we all have a special place in the world, a special kind of work, a calling, that best suits our temperament and talents. Books have been written (the one I remember reading avidly was *Do What You Are*), and success experts have shouted from the rooftops the obvious fact that in order to find fulfilment, to find our rightful place in the world of work, we need to follow our passion. And when we find it, we will be great at our job, dare I say, better than anyone else.

As a result, we start off questioning our current job. Is this really our passion? And if there's anything slightly uncomfortable about our work we tell ourselves that there must be something more attuned to us Out There.

The next obstacle to our performance is that we feel less motivation for our current job and back off a bit. Our attitude changes, becoming a bit more negative and less gung-ho.

Soon we are on the Internet searching for something else, and our focus moves into the future and away from the pressing matters at hand. Nothing has changed about our capabilities or our job. What has changed is our moment-by-moment thinking about it all, framed by the idea that our passion is Out There somewhere waiting to be found. And this thinking absolutely drives our present results. Our performance is an *inside* job, not an outside job.

But before I talk about how to boost your performance from the inside-out, I want to mention another common belief (there you are, another frame!) that says "action equals results, equals performance." Nearly every piece of advice given in our culture seems to say that taking action is the answer to our problems and to great performance. We are told to set hard goals, make a detailed plan of steps and action points over days, months and years to achieve them, and then take massive action to achieve them. And at the end we will feel fulfilled, or something like that.

And so here we all are, rushing around trying to get things done, trying to tick more items off our list, trying to move further along our master plan as quickly as possible. And when we meet a hurdle, we tell ourselves that it's just a part of life, and take more action to climb over it. Then we meet another hurdle, and another, all the while working harder and faster because we are now falling behind our schedule.

What we don't realize is that the hurdles we face are not because something Out There has got in our way. Rather, many of the hurdles we face are there because our inside is sabotaging what we are trying to do on the outside. If we are working all the hours we are given in an effort to improve our performance, while we are actually being controlled by internal frames that don't mesh with the action we are taking, then the frames win every time.

I have always believed that hard work was the way to success, brought about when I achieved a good honors degree through hard, consistent study. I had this image in my mind of dripping water, knowing that if the drip just continues non-stop year after year the rock will slowly change shape. This mindset motivated me to work conscientiously and consistently, always believing that these two qualities would win in place of a few one-off, great performances.

But it didn't work out that way. You see, consistency probably does work well, provided all the other ducks are in a row. However, I also had a frame that said "Be self-sufficient. Don't ever ask for help." And while it is admirable to be conscientious and consistent, in most organizations we don't work in a vacuum; we need to interact with other people a lot to complete our work.

While I worked hard I also worked very much alone, in keeping with my introverted nature, and didn't function well as a team member. I was very much the long-distance runner out there on his own in the hills. At the time, I had no idea I was introverted, as I mentioned earlier, and so I wasn't even aware that I was not playing as a team member. In fact, the interpersonal side of the equation never entered my mind, since I had learned to be conscientious and consistent while studying in the library on my own.

If our frames are actually controlling how we perform as opposed to our outward actions, and if these frames are not in sync with what we are trying to do Out There, then it doesn't matter how hard we try, we will find that our performance suffers. If we really want to get somewhere, then, achieve something challenging or, dare I say it, get rich, the first step is to achieve great performance on the *inside*.

With a strong, powerful engine driving us internally, the work we have to do Out There will come to us with greater ease and will move us forward more powerfully and quickly than any massive action alone will do. You have probably noticed that those who perform at their peak seem to do so without too much strain, with a relaxed state, making it look fairly easy. You will most likely find that the habitual thinking that drives them forward supports their outward intentions and actions perfectly. The solution to great performance, then, is to create great performance on the inside first, and only then work toward great performance on the outside.

How do we create great performance on the inside? If our world, our reality is actually on the inside, in our mind, then it is incumbent upon us to create a wonderful world for ourselves, one that works just for us, that we enjoy every day, that allows us to achieve our dreams. But what's on the inside isn't just our thinking in isolation. When we think, we feel. When I asked you in Chapter

1 to imagine squeezing a lemon's juice into your mouth you probably involuntarily winced. That's the feeling in sync with the thinking. When you see yourself sipping a margarita under the shade overlooking a beach in the Bali I'm sure you don't feel neutral! You may heave a sigh and relax your body slightly and feel wistful.

Yes, we *can* think without having any strong feelings, perhaps when we are being very analytical, but for great performance on the inside we really need to feel. We call this combination of simultaneous thinking and feeling a "state." When we think uplifting thoughts and feel on top of the world, we are in a state that's primed to produce amazing results. We interact with others more confidently and assertively, we analyze and plan our strategy with more clarity, and we see ourselves as more capable and powerful. That's the aim of great performance on the inside.

The key to putting ourselves in a state primed for results is to ensure that great, uplifting frames (beliefs, understandings, decisions etc.) are running our lives, fashioning our reality and making us feel powerful. How do we do this? When we realize that frames that we have assimilated from our families and culture have been running the show and creating our reality all these years without our being aware of them, then the first step is to become *aware* of them.

In Chapter 1 we discussed how we can become aware of the movies in our mind by noticing how we feel and then tracking back to the thought that created it. When we want to identify the frames that create these moment-by-moment thoughts, we start again by looking first at our feelings: "What am I feeling right now as I stand next to Adam? And what am I thinking that's causing me to feel that way?" "I'm feeling nervous because I think Adam is going to criticize me." That's the immediate, moment-by-moment thought.

It pays now to re-visit the concepts we discussed in Chapter 1 and show how they can be used to help us take back control. After thinking, "I'm feeling nervous because I think Adam is going to criticize me," we have another thought about that: "I think Adam is too critical for his own good." It's a second thought that results from our having the first one. And you'd be wrong if you thought it stopped there. We have a third thought based on the second one: "People who criticize a lot are mean."

You may notice that as we go through this process, each subsequent thought becomes less related to the original event, me standing next to Adam, and more up in the air, or conceptual. It's as if we are climbing higher and further away from the original source of our feelings. And as we climb, we make more general statements in our minds and become more emotionally worked up. Our feelings strengthen as we get further away from reality and more into the world of pure concepts, ideas.

The higher we go, the more we enter the realm of frames, those general thoughts that stand for a wide range of situations and that can create a whole host of thoughts and feelings as we make our way through the day. You will notice that the third thought, "People who criticize a lot are mean," is a belief, or a conclusion that can be applied to many people and many situations. This is a frame, and it has the power to direct our thinking, our feelings, our communication and our behavior many times and in many contexts.

With this frame running in our mind, we may be ultra-sensitive to criticism from anyone. Furthermore, we will tend to react negatively to someone who criticizes us, believing they are mean, rather than seeing the communication as helpful feedback from someone who cares about our performance.

Here's a real-life example from my own experience. When I was working in the bank I would often think, "This instruction circular from Head Office that I'm reading is just one more piece of bureaucratic claptrap." But I didn't just think that one thought and be done with it. Oh no! I thought about what I had just thought and concluded, "I should be a bureaucrat to do this job." That's a second thought resulting from the first thought about the instruction circular. And when I said that to myself, I had a further, third thought which was, "I'm not a bureaucrat. I'm more of a marketing man." And this third thought was a frame about my identity.

Now, when I think, "I'm a marketing man," I don't just relate it back to that instruction circular that I was reading. I widen its application to hundreds of different situations, and allow it to create many different moment-by-moment thoughts in each situation. And all those thoughts in all those situations create new feelings, actions and results for me. They literally control my life. This is the power of frames, and the reason why it is essential for us to get hold of them and make them work *for* us instead of allowing them to control us unconsciously.

Let's look at it another way. If we really want to become aware of what is going on inside our mind so that we can take control of it, we need to realize that we think many times over about something. If we pay attention to our consistent thoughts, we invariably find that we come back to a *generalized* thought that covers and influences many aspects of our lives. This is a frame. "People can't be trusted." "When people become managers they change." "At heart, everyone is good." "To succeed in your career you have to be ruthless." "Women make the best bosses." All of these are frames, and within their boundaries are countless thoughts and feelings: horror movies, adventure movies, romance movies that get us emotionally charged and in a state that creates our speech and behavior.

So what about you? What frames are currently in charge of your results? Step back, put some distance between you and your feelings, and get analytical. What am I feeling? How do I feel on a regular basis? What's the underlying tone of my mood each day?

Then, staying in an observer role, dispassionate, get curious about what you are thinking. What is causing me to feel that way? (And no, it is not somebody Out There.) What is habitually running through my mind? What do I keep thinking on and on? How do I repeatedly react to people? What's the thinking behind *that*? And as you go on an internal journey, you will work your way up to the main characters, the ones who drive the drama forward.

Once you have identified the major frames that control your outcomes, it's time to question them. Are they doing me any good? Are they getting in the way of my progress? Identify the sinister ones as well as the heroes. Write them out. Describe what they say to you. And then decide which ones you want to keep, and which ones you want to let go of.

If we substitute the word "belief" for "frame," then we can readily identify which beliefs are limiting us and which beliefs are helping us to move forward and grow. You can substitute the word "conclusion" for "frame" as well. What have I concluded about people and the world, and which conclusions get in the way of my progress, happiness, etc.? Which conclusions have a positive effect on my performance, results, relationships, decisions, happiness, etc.?

You can also substitute other words such as understandings, decisions, or perceptions. A frame is simply a thought that is more general and more consistent, or stuck, than other thoughts. It is a higher level, conceptual thought created by us out of thin air as we think *about* our reactions to the people and events that impact us. And it never leaves our mind if we don't do something about it.

What frames would you like to have on your side? What broad concepts, beliefs, understandings would you like to make up your constant thinking so that they work *for* you instead of against you? It's entirely your choice. Make a list of frames that you would like to have helping you run your life, and choose the one or two that you want most of all. Then start with those. You can now choose those ways of seeing the world that control your decisions, how you relate to people, and how you act out every moment so that you get the results you want.

This is true control, not of people and things, but of yourself. First, of your thinking and feeling, and then of your speech and actions. Once you have absolute control of these four things, you can let the world Out There take care of itself. It will bow to your will, because that world will in fact be yours, the one you choose.

So how do we let go of frames that we no longer want controlling us, and how do we assimilate new ones into our system of thinking? By directing a powerful internal movie of ourselves experiencing the results of our new frame. Powerful because this internal movie gets your juices going, full of emotion and drama (to you). As the new frame takes hold in your mind, the old one, the one you wish to let go of, will naturally slip away as it is replaced by the one that you have a greater need for. It's the internal movie of your new frame that will change the make-up of your thinking. All you need to do is sit back and watch your new internal movie over and over, each time acting out the speech and behavior it inspires.

Let me give you an example. I used to smoke Hamlet cigars. A school friend of mine first introduced me to cigars when I was eighteen. We were having dinner at his parents' house, and after dinner his father took out a box of Cuban cigars. My friend offered me one, and without knowing how to smoke a cigar I took one puff and inhaled deeply, as if I was destined to! The buzz I got from that one inhale set me up for years to come. I inhaled every cigar I smoked from then on until my lungs had had enough when I was about thirty-five.

At that point I decided to quit. My new frame was, "I hate cigars and smoking." I had heard about a thing called visualization, which was all the rage at that time, so I decided to try it myself. I sat quietly in an armchair in my living room and just relaxed. When I was unwound, I closed my eyes and saw, in my mind, myself looking through my eyes and seeing in huge detail right in front of my nose ten enormous lit cigars sticking out of my mouth. I felt myself inhaling them all at once and I then felt the acrid smoke and fire from ten cigars fill my lungs.

As I looked, I saw the red glow of the fire of all the cigars burn brighter right in front of me, and then as I exhaled I saw masses of thick, gray smoke rising up and felt it burning my eyes. And as I exhaled I felt myself coughing deeply and sorely as if my lungs would split. Even though my eyes were still closed and this movie was all in my mind, I started coughing for real.

That movie had an enormous impact on me, and I ran it several times a day for the next week or so. The result was that every time I thought about having a smoke (ran a fabulous movie of the enjoyment of smoking a cigar) that thought, that internal movie, was immediately replaced by the other awful, acrid-tasting movie of the ten cigars. It was so bad that I no longer felt like having a cigar. Therefore, I didn't have one. This pattern continued until a few weeks later the fabulous movie of me smoking a cigar disappeared from my mind, and I no longer had the need for the horror movie. And I have never even felt like smoking since.

The trick is to run the movie in as dramatic a fashion as possible. You can make it close-up, with vivid colors, dramatic action, and strong effects on your emotions. I can't tell you what will stir up your juices and give you strong emotions about a topic. It's entirely up to you to make it very personal and meaningful to you. Internal stuff is just for you. You don't need anybody else telling you how to run your own movies.

To show you that this process doesn't just apply to quitting addictions but can be used to install any frames you like, I'll quickly tell you how I gained unconditional self-acceptance after living most of my life feeling "less than". Quite recently I was sitting in a nice, leather wing back chair in my study just trying to relax, not doing anything. I was staring at the corner of the white wall in front of me when a thought came into my mind: "I'm sitting here in this chair doing nothing, and that's perfectly OK. I'm just fine as I am, just OK. What I think is just OK. And what I say and do is OK. By me. And that's just fine."

I had already primed myself by reading *A Course in Miracles* and other books that talk about us as if we are perfectly OK, so in a way I had already chosen this thought. And I was really, really tired of feeling that other people were somehow more important than me, too busy for me, not to be disturbed, and so on. So this was the new frame I wanted to assimilate, that "I am just OK as I am."

I ran an internal movie of myself moving through the world untouched by the emotions and reactions of others, but turning inward each time I was challenged and relying on my own thoughts about things, my own feelings in response to things, and my own words and actions as I dealt with things. It kind of felt like I had a really good friend backing me up, so that I had the courage to tell people what I really thought and wanted, to speak my truth, instead of getting caught up in their emotional business and expectations.

This movie was full of emotion as well, but of course was in no way similar to the cigar emotion. I felt strong and powerful and supremely comfortable. I felt that at last, I could relax in myself, dwell in myself, and rely absolutely on myself. I felt absolutely OK. No guilt. No need to please others. No feeling that I have done something wrong, let someone down. And this new frame, that "I am just OK as I am," has empowered me to become an author, something I never even thought about during my earlier years.

Let me repeat: internal performance means having the ability and determination to choose and assimilate into our system new frames that positively drive our outward performance forward. What we think about and feel on a regular basis translates into almost automatic speech and behavior and action that create clear results. We can allow destructive frames to control our reality and make our world a certain hell to live and work in. Or we can take charge of our frames and create a driving force that lifts us up and helps us reach the summit of our own personal mountain. That's real performance.

So give yourself a performance review. Review what you think performance is really about, and try turning inwards to discover the magic in your mind that creates all your outcomes. You don't have to spend hours sitting in silence to do this. While looking inside will exercise new mental muscles, you can simply STOP and ask yourself, "What am I feeling and therefore thinking?" at any time during the day. You may just be surprised by what you find.

While uplifting, motivating frames are the essential driving force behind our performance, we still need to do the work Out There in the tangible world. How we define our own personal mountain and adopt the right action plan to climb it will determine how far we succeed in achieving our dreams. So now we turn to the idea of success and how to achieve it. You just may be surprised by the answer.

CHAPTER 4

A SUCCESS

REBOOT

We all want success, don't we? And we all know what we mean by success, don't we? Don't we? We can all see our future success: the big house overlooking the beach; the beautiful or handsome partner; the luxury executive sports sedan; and the healthy bank balance. But in this chapter, I'm afraid I'm going to burst your bubble a bit, and show you a new way to think about success so that you don't ache for years and years, running those internal movies until one day in the distant future, perhaps, you finally make it. As usual, I'll get started with a bit about my own success, or perhaps lack of it.

I remember the first "success" book I ever read. It was

Think and Grow Rich by Napoleon Hill. After reading it, I still had no idea how to think and thereby grow rich, but the idea behind it, that success was something out there to attain, was firmly embedded in the front of my mind. Thus began my search for the holy grail of success, and I soaked up all kinds of books with titles like *The Success Principles and Awaken the Giant Within*.

Success to me meant gaining financial freedom (remember that phrase?) through passionate work, so that I would never have to worry about where the dollars would come from to pay for my expensive tastes. I also saw success as finally, after a long struggle, winning the respect of the people around me. And financial freedom and respect from others would ultimately bring me my own self-respect, freedom from feeling that I was "less than." I would finally be able to tell myself I had made it.

As a result, I began to have a constant feeling that I had not made it yet, that I had quite a long way to go, and that I would have to search for my passion and then work very hard for a long time until I had made enough money to feel worry-free. I had thoughts that I would at a minimum have to start my own business in something that I was naturally talented at and passionate about, and then struggle in a harsh, cut-throat environment until someday I could sit back and go "Whew! Now I can relax and sip margaritas by the beach for the rest of my life." The prospect of all that struggle daunted me and gave me enormous pressure, as if I didn't already have enough.

All for what? All for just an idea, a concept in my and countless other minds. We think that success is tangible, a thing out there in the future or in the world to be worked toward. We look at the word "success" and we automatically decide that that's what we want, without ever thinking deeply about it. Yes, we were advised to create vision boards with pictures of the beautiful location we were going to live in, the specific house we were going to buy, the sports car we were going to own, and the wonderful person we were going to marry. And we had a date by when we would have all this stuck boldly in the middle. But how many of us are truly clear about what success means, apart from being rich? It's a concept that stirs up our emotions just by being what it is, a thought about the future.

Success isn't real. It doesn't exist. It's just a thought. A frame. A very powerful illusion. And this power has the ability to make us feel that we are currently unsuccessful, and that we will remain so until some magical, far off day. We spend years thinking that we are not as good as other people who have already succeeded, feeling inferior and a bit desperate. All the time struggling in the hope that this thing called success will come to us eventually.

That sounds like misery to me. At the end of the day it doesn't mean anything. People who have succeeded have only done so in our mind, whatever we define their success as being. It may also be in their mind, or it may not. We have no way of knowing. And while we keep calling other people successful, we downgrade ourselves, not realizing that these other people's successes are our creation, all ours, all just in our mind. It's like eating a whole box of chocolates and then feeling lousy about ourselves. We did it all by ourselves, to ourselves.

So why don't we redefine the concept of success? Why

hold onto a frame that acts like an addiction? Here's a new frame that I use to find success: "When I connect with what I really want deep down inside and then have the courage to act it out in what I say and do, then I am successful." I find that this ability to stop and listen to my true wants and then use that knowledge to lead me through the day gives me a feeling of tangible movement forward and power.

I call the voice I listen to my "inner guide," but you can call it your second level thought, your intuition, your spirit, your true self or whatever. It comes to us all day long. All we have to do is notice it in challenging situations and respond to it instead of doing a knee-jerk reaction and saying or doing what our busy, caught-up-in-the-situation mind tells us. In my case, my knee-jerk reaction is usually to hurry to prevent conflict or to make sure the other person doesn't feel uncomfortable. This is in direct contradiction to what my inner guide might tell me.

This new concept of success as being a series of many, small, moment-by-moment or day-by-day successes that positively move our work and life forward, isn't any less powerful than the old, pressure cooker one. It gives you a feeling of achievement and power every day. You don't have to wait for it. And rather than setting tough goals five years ahead and planning each step to get there, here we let the future more or less take care of itself.

We know we are moving forward in the right direction because on a micro level we are following our wants all the time, so at the end of the day we make progress toward what we want to achieve anyway. But instead of imagining what we want in the form of far-away goals, we are more certain that we are on the right path because we are paying attention to our wants and needs continually in real time.

I know now that the goals for success that I set for myself years ago are totally irrelevant to me today, and I'm glad I never achieved them. Not only that, I feel good about myself every day as I don't compare myself to others who have succeeded. They have a different path and good luck to them. My path is mine alone, full of anticipation and excitement. This, then, is the frame that I have decided to use to give me more control over my performance and destiny. It's a concept up there in my mind that creates my decisions and actions on the ground.

Now let's get down and dirty with the stuff happening on the ground. You remember when I was working in banking I had this frame of my ideal Self as a marketing-cum-businessman, a dynamic person working away from the office most of the time, making deals and being gregarious? This frame kept me firmly planted in the "keep searching until you find your passion" camp, in the future, where I expected to find work I truly loved and was meant to do.

As a result, I was not really there at my job, focused on the work in front of me as much as I needed to be. I didn't value it, and so I worked in a half-hearted way, doing what I was supposed to do, not letting people down, but not performing at my best. Furthermore, I let my emotions enter my work too much, feeling all kinds of negative feelings of frustration and anger which made me miserable and even more disconnected. And as my performance suffered, I grew even more despondent because I felt trapped in a job I thought I didn't fit into.

Once again, I had it all wrong. As I looked back in later years I realized the value of pure concentration and hard work. I did not succeed as a top student because I was fascinated by economics. In fact, I was more fascinated by languages and Spanish in particular, and had spent my gap year in Spain studying the language at a university there. The reason I decided to study economics back in Scotland was simply that I thought it would be more useful for the world of business, especially if I could speak Spanish. My decision was not to follow my passion, but to be utterly practical, since I knew I didn't want to be a teacher or professional linguist but wanted to enter the world of business in some way.

I dedicated myself to learning economics, and as I studied and worked at the subject I became more and more engrossed in it and began to love it. As I understood it more, as the big picture of what it was all about slowly came into my awareness, I loved it more. And finally, by my final exams at the end of four years, I understood how all the parts fitted together, how the system worked, and I felt wonderful! It seemed natural that I went into banking, and so that's what I did, as you remember.

The lesson from this story is that happiness and fulfilment from your work doesn't necessarily come from finding that one job that you feel you are best suited to. Some people may be natural doctors or academics and find a fit, but I suspect that the majority of us will keep searching and searching and never really know where their rightful place is, if there is one at all.

I further suspect that even if you always knew you wanted to be a doctor and were passionate about it at the outset, if you don't get really serious about constantly improving and building up your knowledge and skills to be the very best you can be, you may find yourself in a rut, feeling a little worn, and underperforming. The truth, as I found out at university, is that dedication to the craft you are engaged in right in front of you is the surest way to find passion at work, not searching the world of work to find your passion.

There's a word in Sanskrit, "dharma," which cannot be directly translated into English, and which has many meanings. But as far as work is concerned, it can mean duty, good works, character, quality or ethics, and to me means focusing like a laser on the job at hand and creating the best quality you possibly can, the best performance you are capable of. This word encompassing the idea that doing good work as your duty is so important that it is given a full chapter in Chin Ning Chu's book *Thick Face Black Heart* about Asian psychology applied to business.

As we focus and work conscientiously, we learn. To perform at our best, we need to make a strong decision to build up our skills and knowledge and to become highly competent at what we do. And from my own experience, competence breeds pride, a feeling of personal power, and enjoyment of the work. Put simply, when you are really good at what you do, you feel great.

Cal Newport, in his frame-changing book *So Good They Can't Ignore You*, tells us that Self-Determination Theory—the theory of what really motivates us—

identifies three basic psychological needs in order for us to get a kick out of our work: Autonomy, Competence and Relatedness.

By Autonomy, we mean the ability to determine your path, which comes from being given more responsibility as you climb the organization ladder. Perhaps that's why so many people crave starting their own business. They want to be their own boss, to have the autonomy it brings.

Competence means being really good at your work. If you become an expert at what you do by focusing on what is in front of you and building your skills, you will most likely start liking your job more and will probably get more autonomy as you gain more responsibility. That's a double whammy.

And finally, Relatedness means having good relationships with those around you at work, feeling that you are a member of a team and working together to achieve outcomes. And it's my suspicion that your relationships at work may just improve when you show your competence and become a more valuable member of the team.

The title of Cal Newport's book, *So Good They Can't Ignore You,* is a frame. It's a concept that we can assimilate into our everyday consciousness to drive our performance. Within this frame lie multiple thoughts and feelings that cause us to focus hard, work assiduously and keep learning so that we gradually build what Cal calls "career capital." With career capital, we have power and freedom. Now, instead of searching for our passion, we have the value embedded in our skills, knowledge and experience that enable us to move into other areas of work when we feel ready.

This time we don't leave our present job because we dislike it, but we leave in order to take advantage of an opportunity that moves us higher. Our move is for a positive, affirming reason rather than for a negative, desperate reason. With this frame, building career capital is the new objective, rather than finding our fit or starting our own business. These things may come, but only after we have given ourselves the true respect brought about by supreme competence.

It looks like we're back to frames, doesn't it? It doesn't matter how much we dwell on the real world out there—the tough, rubber meets the road stuff—we always seem to come back to our internal stuff. This is truly a paradigm change from the common understandings we have lived with all these years. The idea that performance and success must start with what is going on inside us is not new in the world, in fact it has been known over the ages. But it is new for us, in our fast and furious business culture where it's considered dangerous to stop and think too much, where action trumps contemplation.

I'm not asking you to become a seer who sits and ponders all day. I'm asking you to become aware of the real forces influencing your results, the thinking patterns that project outwards onto people and events and create your reality and behavior. It's no longer acceptable to live unconsciously, letting unseen forces in your head direct your destiny and sabotage your well-meaning efforts.

It's time to take back control by identifying the frames that are currently running the show and asking if they are doing you any good, and by consciously choosing new frames that give you the power to overcome challenges with resilience and succeed entirely on your own terms.

To me, then, success comes from being true to your Self by identifying what you really, really want and having the courage to speak your truth in every moment, while using "dharma" to create the career capital that will propel you higher and higher. And, of course, just letting the future take care of itself.

So far, we have been talking about performance and success. But we don't perform in a vacuum. We need to work with other people in order to achieve the outcomes we want. It's no good living in your head all day long and ignoring those around you. If we want to have positive, effective dealings with others we need to understand how our relationships really work. That's the subject of the next chapter.

CHAPTER 5

A PEOPLE

MAKEOVER

Dealing with other people at work can make or break a career. Especially when we feel that we have no power and no say and that others somehow control us, from the hours we work to our happiness.

When we work in a big corporation, we think that we are small and unimportant and have to play by others' rules. These rules are not laws passed by any Government, but are mostly unspoken givens that announce that we are a part of the team, that we are fully paid up members of the corporate culture. Even if we run our own business, there are accepted ways of doing business in "this industry", and don't hope to get any clients if you step outside of them.

We perceive these rules as being real things out there that can be touched, facts about how we must behave. Consequently, we defer to them and make our company our emperor. The truth is, there's nothing and nobody out there controlling us. This may come as a surprise to those of you stuck in a cubicle, but this chapter will give you some hope and some methods that will dismantle this empire just like the Roman one. And to introduce you to these, let me tell you ...

My first responsibility in the bank was managing customer services of a branch in a country in the Middle East. I was twenty-five and pretty green. I had not yet learned to trust my instincts, and so when my immediate boss stopped me writing letters to my customers in mid-flow and wrote them himself, I thought he knew better. I was annoyed that he didn't think I was capable of writing a simple customer letter, but then he was much older than me and I assumed he knew exactly what he was doing.

However, when it came to signing the letters, it was my signature that went on them and I was not too happy to be sending the messages he wrote under my name. The way he expressed himself to customers was different from the way I expressed myself. I should have said something, because in my gut this didn't feel right. But because he was my boss I let it go even though I did not agree with it.

This was just a small matter in the broad scheme of things, but is representative of a much wider and more sinister pattern in companies where the boss is not questioned by those under him about actions and behavior which may not be ethical or appropriate. The whole 2008 banking crisis is an example of this kind of pattern run riot. For us, this pattern of not questioning things gives our power away to others. And it is all our fault. People don't exercise power over us by force; they are given it freely by us, and they willingly accept it.

How do we do this? We create this powerful person ourselves, in our mind, and then assume that is just the way they are. We see them as a fixed personality, a fact, a still image, all of their own making, and thus blame them for the way they are.

The truth is that we take one behavior and apply it to them as if it represents the whole person. My boss in the Middle East talked with a sharp tongue in the office and didn't listen very much, and so I created an entire person out of that behavior. I saw him as domineering and insensitive, even wicked, but always powerful, and this creation of mine dominated my relationship with him for two years. It affected the way I responded to him, which was with compliance colored with resentment and anger. All unexpressed, of course. And it made me miserable and less effective at my job. The truth is, he was none of those things. It was all my own creation.

We are very good at generalizing. It helps us keep a complex world simple and comprehensible. But when we take someone's thirty seconds of behavior and say to ourselves, "That's who she is," then our generalizing can ruin our chances of working effectively with that person.

Often, we give away our power by feeling like we did when we were small and seeing the other person as one of our parents, unaware that we are projecting our history onto the person in front of us. This can happen when the person in front of us says or does something that reminds us of a behavior one of our parents did years ago. A terse remark by a colleague in a meeting can set off a firework display of thoughts and emotions that we used to have twenty years before.

Most of the time this happens out of our awareness, just a program running in the background. In fact, the behavior doesn't even have to be the exact same way one of our parents behaved. We might perceive the other person's behavior as being "something my father did" when in fact it is quite different. Our internal "stuff" has enormous power when it comes to dealing with people. I owe my understanding of this concept to David Richo and his revelatory book *When the Past is Present: Healing the Emotional Wounds That Sabotage Our Relationships.*

When it comes to protecting ourselves and standing up to people, it is wise to realize that this ogre, this powerful person we perceive in front of us, is actually an illusion, a mere thought that we have conjured up as a result of a myriad of different influences throughout our life. Whew! What a relief! We no longer have to be scared or even nervous and supplicant around him. He is not who we think he is. He just is. A piece of clay waiting for us to play with and form into someone identifiable. (I have to thank Michael Neill for this clay metaphor. He talks about using the "play dough of Thought" in his life-transforming book *The Space Within: Finding Your Way Back Home.*

And what we do with that piece of clay can scare the hell out of us or it can leave us confident and strong.

It is entirely within our own hands. What he thinks of himself is irrelevant because we will never really know—all we have to go on is his behavior, his speech and actions, and they can not only change from moment to moment, but can be interpreted in as many different ways as there are people on this planet. None of it is fixed, a fact, real.

If we want to have personal power in the company of others, all we need to do is manage our thoughts about them in such a way that we do not see them as more powerful than us. Yes, they may be able to decide whether we keep our job or not, but that is a part of their responsibility in their role as our boss, not a reason for us to be scared or to act in opposition to what we think is right. If we perceive them as "just is," without all the baggage from our internal stuff, then we are free to flex our responses according to the situation and what we think is right for us or for the team. We are able to remain open-minded and relaxed, with our emotions chugging along in neutral.

Again, this is all within our control, within our own power. In order to perceive another person as "just is", we need to step back, dissociate from them, get psychological distance. Most of the time our emotions get out of whack because we personalize another person's behavior, feeling that what she says is personal to us and critical of us. Sometimes we interpret every tone of voice and choice of word as a slight against us, thereby setting us up for an emotional hijacking and an internal movie of the person we are dealing with disliking, disrespecting and attacking us.

When we step back in our mind and see our colleague as just a person, then we can become an observer, a curious bystander, who notices their behavior dispassionately as if studying it, rather than seeing them as a persecutor, a bully or a difficult person with all our attendant feelings. And as a curious observer we are in a position to learn about them and better understand what really makes them tick.

So rather than feeling at the mercy of other people, victims of their personalities and power plays, we can adopt the frame, "I am an observer of people and I like to learn about them" and move forward without anxiety about dealing with them. This neutral, analytical mindset dispels all the emotional heaviness around working with others, and leaves us free to concentrate on what *we* want and how to respond accordingly.

We no longer carry weighty expectations, thoughts about people as being "nice" or "forthcoming" or "helpful" and then get angry when they don't live up to them. No longer do we see others as "mean," "selfish" or "secretive" and then interpret all their behaviors under these negative umbrellas. We act as Jiu jitsu masters, flexing our responses, yielding, being supple and pliable in our behavior, in playing out a strategy, a technique of dissociation and observation.

As we learn more and more each time we interact with them, noticing the range of behaviors they employ, the more we gain power over our interpersonal strategies. We can adapt to others' patterns more quickly and choose responses that better bring us the results that we desire. In this way, we gradually gain more and more control over our dealings with our colleagues, our clients and our leaders, and as we do this we move our career or our business forward in the direction *we* want, not what others want.

In this chapter, we have talked a lot about interpersonal power and ways of perceiving others so that we don't give our own power away. But there's more to dealing with people than just seeing them differently. We have to engage with them in a way that enables us to keep our power and get the help we need from them, when we need it most. And this is why the art of communication is so important. If you want to learn how to be a great communicator with loads of influence, turn to the next chapter.

CHAPTER 6

A COMMUNICATION RESTATEMENT

Many books have been written about influence. It's something we all wish we had more of. And it's one of those concepts that just frustrates the hell out of us as we struggle to "influence" somebody.

It's common knowledge that you'll never get what you want if you keep doing what you've always done. Well that sums up communication and influence in a nutshell. We can't help it. We just keep pushing our stuff at other people more and more assertively and louder and louder, and assume that the light bulb will eventually go on in them. But it never does. So why don't we try a different approach? That's what this chapter is all about. And to launch us into this frustrating but satisfying topic, I've got a short example to give you.

I remember listening to a speaker at a business convention a few years ago. He talked and talked, and never noticed that people were getting agitated and losing interest. He just kept talking with the same style and content, looking straight in front of him, totally oblivious to his audience. He somehow thought that just going through his prepared presentation was enough to communicate his message. Eventually people started voting with their feet.

This sounds like an extreme example of poor communication, but it is symptomatic of what most of us do on a regular basis. We try to influence others by talking at them, not with them. We think that if we just say what is in our mind loud and strong enough, the other person will magically "get it." I try to communicate my point of view to you, as if I am somehow injecting a special serum into you that causes you to exclaim "Ah! Yes! Now I get it!"

We think that communication occurs Out There, somewhere in the ether, and is merely a question of transmission, of sending my message over to you. This is the common model that students of communication are taught: sender-message-receiver. It's as if I, as receiver of your message, will just take it in and assimilate it into my understanding and acceptance. No wonder it never works. How many times have you tried to get your opinion across to somebody else and been frustrated at your lack of success, blaming your colleague for not understanding? We always seem to blame the receiver for not having the smarts to understand what is in our mind.

The truth is, what goes on Out There in the ether has very little to do with communication. The sending of my words over to you so that you can hear them does not constitute communication. What *does* constitute communication is what goes on In Here, in our minds as we come into contact with each other.

The moment I set my eyes upon you, communication starts. I am thinking, "Oh no, here comes that jerk!" or "Great, John is coming over." Stuff that I have inside me comes to the surface and affects the way I am thinking about you. It may not be fair and it may even have nothing to do with you because it is all my stuff, but the fact is I am waiting for your words with a frame about you already fixed in my head. And you had better believe that that frame controls the way I interpret and understand what you have to say to me.

Similarly, when you see me you will have fixed thoughts about me, what kind of person I am and how you feel about me. Nothing is neutral. We don't start with a blank slate waiting for someone to write on. We have a kaleidoscope in our heads, and if you think a single message from someone is going to be noticed among all the shapes and colors, you have another think coming! If I am somehow programmed to think that you are not reliable, then no matter how well you present your case, I will not accept it. If I already have it in my mind that another colleague is a jerk, stories of how he helps people will not influence me.

But it doesn't stop there. I don't only have fixed ideas about you and other people that color my reception of your message, but since my whole world resides inside my mind, I have a fixed idea about what constitutes reality. And you are not going to convince me otherwise by trying to transmit your reality to me. It's yours, and has nothing to do with me. I will never see your world, your reality, if you just talk to me about it. When you talk to me about how *you* see things, I will immediately interpret your message in accordance with *my* reality, *my* frames, *my* way of seeing things. I will distort it to allow it to enter my world, and that distortion will be nothing to do with your thinking, which you are trying to get across to me.

What is really going on here is that my inner stuff is coming into contact with your inner stuff, which makes for a very complex mix. I may have a frame that tells me that the way to move the project forward is to push everyone as hard as possible, taking immediate action without wasting a second. This will translate into the way I speak to my team members, probably short and sharp with things for people to do straight away. I don't know where this frame comes from, but it probably goes back quite a long way.

My colleague, on the other hand, has a frame that says it is sensible to discuss and check possible consequences before jumping into the fire. She advocates doing due diligence before taking action, and may express her viewpoint in slower, more measured speech about possible failure. Again, this frame may come from way back.

Here we have a classic opportunity for conflict, and I don't think either party will agree on the best way forward. This meeting of inner stuff is the crux of why communication is so hard, and why we get so frustrated when we try to "get" someone else to understand how we see things and what we think is the right thing to do.

In addition we need to use words, tone and body language to get our reality across to the other person. Words are just symbols we use to represent what we want to say, to send our thinking and emotions out into the world. But they can only ever be an approximation to the complexity of what is going on with us. They generalize our thinking and feeling, package it into a format that can be easily spoken. Words like "bad" or "nice" are poor representations of what we really mean when we use them.

Furthermore, they can be interpreted by the receiver in any number of ways, and a myriad of assumptions and conclusions and pictures and movies can arise out of just one word like "bad." The business word I like is "associate," as in "He's my associate." This is the perfect word to use when you don't want the listener to know the exact relationship between you and the person you're with. They can create any meaning out of it that they like.

The meaning we apply to words we hear will depend on what is going on inside of us, as does the meaning of a certain tone of voice or facial expression. We think that our words and expressions are universally understood, that they have a fixed meaning that everybody knows; but the truth is, people's history and unique programming predisposes them to their own interpretations, resulting in emotions and reactions that we didn't expect. No wonder there's so much misunderstanding. I suspect that if people really knew how complex communication was, they would be a lot more tolerant when they don't succeed in getting their message across.

Why, then, do we give people's words so much power? If we are not careful, we can allow somebody to make us feel really small and unimportant just by perceiving their words as fact, as the truth. We run the risk of being influenced to think, feel and do things that do us no good, all on the back of a word somebody utters to us.

But words don't actually have any power if we don't assign it to them. They are merely sound waves or ink on a piece of paper or light on a screen. What happens after we hear or read them is all inside our own minds. We create meaning out of these symbols that can lift us up or destroy us.

We need to understand this: the power of somebody's words has nothing to do with them and everything to do with us. We are responsible for how we respond to somebody's communication. It is all within our own hands; we have the ultimate power to make whatever meaning, and hence whatever feeling and action, we like out of what somebody says or writes to us. Again, communication is mostly an inside job. It is about how we create our reality as a result of our receiving a message from somebody. They are unable to change our reality with their message; only we can do that.

So how can we have more influence with people, be better at communicating important understandings and intentions so that we and the other person come to a common understanding about the way forward?

Well, we already know that this is not achieved by trying to push our reality onto them, to tell them what we are thinking and expect them to understand and accept it. If we cannot hope to influence another person by forcing our frames onto them, then it stands to reason that we need to work with *their* frames, *their* reality, and forget about ours.

Let's start with a question: What is the purpose of communication? To get others to think like we do? So many people attempt to do this and fall flat on their faces, and in the meantime negatively affect the relationship they have with the other person. We will never get another person to think like we do! So, let's not even try.

A more practical purpose might be to get somebody to feel a certain way, and thereby take some action that would benefit the project or move the work forward. We know that state drives action, and action produces results. It's no good getting somebody to listen to us if nothing happens as a result. Even if this communication is only in terms of having a better relationship, some kind of action will ultimately take place to improve on the present situation. And a change in state in another person will only happen through the medium of *their* frames and *their* internal movies. We have to get inside their head.

I remember being in a sales meeting with the HR manager of a large oil company, trying to persuade her to buy my course on communication skills when I was a corporate trainer. There were just the two of us on opposite sides of a large desk, and while our positioning was not great, as we talked and listened an understanding began to arise. As she talked, I began to sense what she was thinking and going to say next. I felt like I was just ahead of her, and I found myself talking about things that she was just on the verge of talking about. I almost forgot what I had come to say, and entered a conversation all about what her perspective was, how she saw things and felt about things, and where she wanted to go next. I noticed the kinds of words she used and used them myself, and I followed her way of sitting and generally being there. Rather than being a stressful, forced meeting, it turned out to be a calm, relaxed meeting, enjoyable for both parties. And I got the business.

Most of what I did in that meeting was instinctive, but it pays to pay attention and observe how people are. When you observe from a neutral standpoint you can learn about the other person's frames from the things they talk about and the things that engage their emotions. You can look to their history and, just like you did with yourself in Chapter 2, identify patterns of behavior and how they regularly spend their time. This, of course, can only take you so far.

For me, by far the best tool is to get out of myself when I am in somebody's company and sense how they are feeling and what they are thinking, a kind of sixth sense that we all have. We may be wrong some of the time, but I have found that I can connect with others on their terms when I use this sense. The lesson is that we need to stop pushing our agenda at others, thinking that if we can just work out a better way to get our stuff across, then the other person will understand the way we understand, feel the way we feel, and do what we want them to do.

Of course, there's no guarantee that, even if you do become aware of how the other person sees things, you will succeed in your communication. The best lesson I have come across in helping me to succeed with my communication is the NLP presupposition, "The meaning of your communication is the response you get." (NLP means Neuro-Linguistic Programming and is an area of thought and practice that helps people achieve change in their lives.) This presupposition says that it doesn't matter what message you wanted to get across, the only message that matters is the one that the other person received.

You can only know what that message is by noticing how they respond to your communication: their facial expression, their body language, and what they say and do. How they respond tells you what meaning they are working with. And that is the only meaning that counts. Therefore, if you didn't intend the other person to respond in the way that they do, you have to try to communicate your meaning again, and again, all the while understanding that they will never see things in exactly the same way you do.

This strategy of flexing your communication to move closer and closer to mutual understanding shows respect for the differences in perception between the two of you, and acknowledges their world view as well as yours. You speak, watch, listen and learn. And when you know that the meaning the other person has created in their mind is different from the meaning you intended to communicate, then you adapt your own speech, voice and body language so that you move further into their understanding of how the world works, their frames.

As you use words and expressions that resonate with them, and match the way they are in voice and body language, then they will begin to understand what you are trying to communicate and you will be able to influence them toward, not the way you think, but the state and action you desire them to experience.

It is essential that we understand that being able to influence people requires that we appreciate how differently they see the world from us: how different their thinking, their re-presentation of what's Out There is from our own. And in the case of communication, what's Out There is what we say and how we behave as we interact with them. They are nothing like us, and we will keep banging our heads against a brick wall if we insist that they should understand us based on telling them the story from our point of view.

But if we get out of our own head and use our powers of observation and imagination to get a peek at their way of seeing the world, at the reality that they have created in their mind, then we have the key to getting them on our side and taking the action that we need them to take. We can then talk their talk and walk their walk and move forward in lockstep.

In this book, we have talked about using a new way of thinking about ourselves and our world to overcome the challenges we face: in our feelings about ourselves and our careers, in our performance at work, in succeeding in our careers, in dealing with the people on our team, and in communicating with, and influencing, others to cooperate with us and help us.

But there is one final piece of the jigsaw puzzle that I have learned about through harsh experience and which is critical to our success, our fulfilment, and our happiness. Turn the page and you will learn about making the kinds of decisions that can set us on a path of joy and satisfaction or condemn us to years of purgatory.

CHAPTER 7

A DECISION

SHIFT

One choice can change your whole life, for better or worse. Think back to the big decisions you have made in your life. What were the consequences in every aspect of your life? How long did it take you to fully understand those consequences? Do you now look back many years later with regret? Or are you delighted with the decisions you made? Did you feel relief or excitement? Were you running away from something or moving toward a new goal? And did you feel that the decision was just right for you, or was it to appease other people? Whatever we decide, what is indisputable is that the decision will most likely have a high impact and wide repercussions down the road for us and those around us. I should know.

I decided to give up an international banking career at the age of thirty-two. And looking back from today's perspective, it was the wrong decision. You will already know that when I was working in banking I thought it wasn't dynamic or exciting enough for me, that I would be more suited to a career in marketing or running my own business. I had this false sense of my Self as an extrovert who was gregarious and good with people.

This was a frame, a catch-all belief about myself that created a whole basket of negative thoughts about my daily work in the bank and the status and competence of my employer. And it was this belief, rather than any rational or intuitive input into the decision, that totally ran the show. I just knew I had to find my passion, whatever that was, and so I left with no job to go to and no real idea of what kind of employment I was best suited to, other than one meant for a marketing or businessman type.

The psychologist Daniel Kahneman, author of the book *Thinking Fast and Slow*, theorized that a person's decision-making is the result of a combination of our rational thought and intuition working together to produce the outcome. As far as rational thought is concerned, most of us first turn to what we can analyze out there in terms of advantages and disadvantages, pros and cons, or benefits and costs of making the decision.

We define the problem as far as we understand it, then we choose our criteria for making the right decision, then we look at the alternative roads we can take, and finally we choose one of the roads based on our aforementioned benefits and costs etc. We think we are being thorough in our analysis and are convinced that this will lead to the one right decision.

What we don't realize is that even the very first step, defining the problem, is colored by our world-view, our frames. We can define a problem in any number of ways, depending on how we think about it, how we interpret it. My problem in the bank, so I thought, was that I was not suited to that kind of career. This frame then colored my criteria: I wanted a career away from desk-work, and with less focused analysis and more interpersonal contact. Therefore, the alternatives I gave myself were "stay" or "leave."

But if I had defined my problem differently, the whole decision may have been different. If I had dug just a little deeper into my patterns of thinking and doing, I would have realized that I was more of a dreamer than an action person. I would have realized that my thoughts about working in marketing or business were just dreams I had conjured up due to my father being in business on his own and his secretary's shock at learning that I was going into banking.

The lesson I have now learned is that my decision was framed by my erroneous belief about who I was and what I was like. In other words, it didn't matter how much rational thought I applied to the decision, or how much my emotions swayed me, the decision to leave banking was made above and beyond all the analysis and feeling.

I was being driven by an unseen force, insofar as I was not aware of it, and this force was far too powerful for analytics, pros and cons and possible future consequences. I can only conclude that our decisions are not what they seem; that we are driven by our beliefs, understandings, assumptions and conclusions in the form of frames that are out of our awareness, and that this unseen force shapes any conscious effort we make to choose the right path.

This is all beginning to get monotonous, isn't it? It doesn't seem to matter how much we think we are in control of our destiny, or how hard we work to take control, we keep coming back to the same premise: that our external situation is controlled by our internal situation. If we truly want to take charge of our destiny, we have to stop letting our frames control us because we don't notice them, and start paying attention to what we are thinking on a moment-by-moment basis. Furthermore, we have to accept that what we are thinking controls how we feel and what we consequently do, from screwing up our face at someone to quitting a valuable career.

However, the good news is that the kind of control you will feel when you are in charge of your frames is beyond any kind of control you might have Out There. I don't care if you are the CEO of a multinational firm or the Assistant to the Assistant Manager, when you take control of your mind you feel that the world is at your feet.

Which it actually is, since it is your world to do with exactly as you please. When you are aware of the frames that govern your thinking, feeling and doing, and choose which ones you will allow in and which ones you will banish, you are free to become whoever you want. By choosing the overriding thinking you want to operate by, you will sense a freedom to run your own show that nobody else can confer upon you.

And so, if our choices are controlled by our frames, what do we do? We stop letting them control us by becoming aware of them and understanding how they are affecting our decisions. And the first step, which is the reason I wrote this book, is to realize the game that we are playing. To realize that life isn't about what we see going on in the outside world as neutral observers who then decide what to do from a rational standpoint. Instead, we need to realize that frames, which we may call beliefs or conclusions or ways of understanding things, are the main players in the game of life.

Let's now talk about a higher and more powerful frame that has controlled my life at work for years. For most of my life I had the belief that other people at work didn't like to be disturbed because they were far too busy. This belief was permanently in the back of my mind, kind of running there like an operating system. It was a frame because it encompassed and created a whole host of moment-by-moment thoughts, decisions, feelings and actions.

If I had to make a phone call to get someone else in the office to do something for me, I would immediately run a movie in my mind of the person working busily at his desk, picking up the phone in a huff, and answering with a hurried and impatient tone. I would then see myself fumbling my words because I was aware of how upset he was, and ending the conversation without getting what I wanted and damaging the relationship. This was all in my mind, and was so strong that I usually didn't make the call and made do without the help. And, of course, my performance suffered as a result.

You can see in this example how the movie I ran in my mind (the thinking I was doing) totally controlled my destiny Out There. And there were many other movies that ran inside that frame at different times until I decided, many years later, to break it apart and banish it for good. That one frame controlled nearly all my decisions when it came to approaching people, asking for advice or guidance or help, getting on the phone for any reason, and contacting prospects. And I thought I should be in marketing? Well, perhaps, if I had banished that frame long ago.

Let me repeat: we are not destined from a young age to be in a certain career or to be a certain kind of person. We are programmed to be those things, but not destined. We all have the ability to re-program ourselves and start each year, even each day, with a clean slate. We can banish frames (beliefs, conclusions, etc.) that drive us to make decisions that harm us. At the same time, we can put new frames in our mind that make us feel resourceful, capable and confident, and that can help us make decisions that make us happy, successful, rich, content, respected, you name it.

So, what frames can help us make better decisions? It's really up to you what frames you choose to incorporate as a part of your being, but here are two that I now use to make all my decisions, and that I have found give me the most personal power and sense of freedom and control:

"Every decision I make is my own alone and is perfectly OK with me, whatever others may think."

"I trust my inner guide to lead me to the right decision

for me every time."

The first frame is about self-acceptance, which I talked about in Chapter 2. When I go through the day accepting who I am right now, just as I am, whatever anyone else might think or say, I can relax and feel the power of being able to think, say and do whatever I choose and know that that is OK with me, and that I am the only one who counts here.

Obviously, I don't use this belief to be overtly nasty or abusive to others, and I still feel guilty if somebody is actually hurt by my words or actions. In general, however, I believe that people choose to feel what they feel by creating thoughts of their own, even if these thoughts are triggered by something I said or did. It really doesn't matter what my actions were because they were free to interpret them, to think about them, in any way they liked. They weren't forced to think about them in a negative way and feel upset or angry. That was entirely their choice (or rather, it was their frames that led them to have those thoughts).

This frame gives me enormous power, because as I acknowledge that every decision I make is mine and mine alone for reasons only I know about, then I am at cause in everything that happens to me. I choose the path to take. It is my choice and my path, and thus I own it and am the person who created it. With this in mind, I run the show, I am totally in charge of my destiny, and it is entirely my responsibility. I'm in absolute control.

This frame of self-acceptance leads into the second frame, the inner guide. When I accept that I am at cause in my decisions and they are my decisions alone, then I can trust my own instincts to guide me forward. When I say instincts, I am also saying intuition, inner guide, spirit, sense of certainty, connecting with your true self, and so on. But we have to be careful. A strong frame can mislead us into thinking that some of our thoughts are intuition, when they are just highly automated thoughts that arise very quickly as a result of the frame. When I ran the frame that I was unsuited to banking, I had many thoughts about my future that felt like intuition when in fact they were just automatic, knee-jerk thoughts on the back of this all-consuming idea about myself.

What I mean by inner guide is a deeper, stronger and more certain knowing about yourself or something else that arises in the background as you are thinking busy thoughts in the foreground. Some people say we need to become quiet or meditate in order to allow these deeper thoughts, this sense of what is absolutely right for us, to come to us. But I experience them all day long, especially in the middle of a conversation or at a time when I am busily thinking about a decision.

If I'm talking or listening to someone, I will have surface, "busy" thoughts about what we are conversing about, but at the same time other thoughts will come to me from somewhere else, somewhere deeper where my true wants and opinions are located. I know the difference between these deeper thoughts and the surface thoughts because the deeper thoughts will give me the sense of "Yes! That's what I really think!" or "Actually, that's what I really would like to do!" as if they were lying under my surface thoughts.

And my surface thoughts seem to function as a kind of

social grease just to deal with the momentary situation. For me, those surface thoughts are all about how I can please the other person, give them what they want and avoid conflict. But underneath all that my true self is telling me what I am really like and what I really want. That's my inner guide, and that's who I now rely on to guide me to make just the right decisions for me.

My inner guide surfaces all the time if I will just pay attention. It always seems to come to me when I am wrestling with some kind of decision and I am thinking a lot of busy thoughts, weighing up options and adding up advantages and disadvantages. Suddenly a flash of insight will light up my mind and if I'm sharp I will catch it and use it to tell me my true path.

The truth is, however, that while I do become aware of my inner guide informing me, I often don't let it lead me. I ignore it and pay attention to what's going on immediately in front of me. Then I make a decision based on influence from the person opposite me or on a frame that has passed its "use by" date. I'm sure you have also had moments when you just knew from somewhere inside what the right course of action should be, but you overrode it and decided on a path that was easier or more expedient or more acceptable, more in keeping with the common wisdom and corporate culture.

If you really want to feel in control of your destiny, start noticing when your inner guide is bringing you these deeper thoughts, samples of your true Self, the person who is always there in the background looking after you while you tackle office and career challenges.

Listening to and acting on your inner guide moment

by moment will lead you forward in just the right direction for you. It will not help you predict the future because there is no such thing. It will only move you step by step, decision by decision, while allowing your destiny to unfold slowly and naturally, like a flower opening. Instead of deciding based on probability theory ten years down the road, just allow the future to take care of itself while paying attention to what is most important for you right here and now.

CHAPTER 8

A TOUCH ON THE IGNITION

The other day I was watching an episode of *Billions* on TV in which Wendy Rhoades, the in-house performance coach at Axe Capital, was giving a talk to a group of gung-ho financial executives. When she asked them questions, they came back with bravado and hubris, pumping up their image and showing off in front of each other. It was all a big macho game for the boys, who were desperate to get one up on each other: a body-building competition for money people.

Although this was a bit extreme, it nevertheless reminded me of the power game that takes place every day in offices throughout the world, where each player uses fast, aggressive speech to talk himself up in front of team mates and bosses. And, so they think, the fastest and most aggressive talker gets power over the rest.

In the corporate world, it's all about being visible, having a powerful personal brand, getting noticed by those who matter. As the game gets louder and louder, the value of the underlying work suffers as energy is put into image and promotion. Don't we all lap up those books and courses teaching us how to be master presenters? All the while, nobody notices the quiet worker toiling away silently in the background, focusing on his strategy to produce top quality value. He has no need to shout from the rooftops because he feels strong inside, secure in knowing who he is and what he can offer. And he goes by names like Warren Buffet, Bill Gates, or Mark Zuckerberg.

After listening to the executives rant on for a while, Wendy Rhoades said you don't need a "psychological Viagra" (talking yourself up) to pump yourself up. That won't get you where you want to go. All you need is internal strength and toughness. "You have to be strong as steel," she said.

That strength is the source of all your personal power and future progress, and it comes from having absolute control of yourself: what you create in your mind, the states you put yourself in, and all your speech and action. There's no need to try and get one up on the person next to you, work late at night so that others can see your dedication, or make a killing presentation to a client. What matters is your delivery, pure and simple.

How many times have we all watched or read advertisements from well-known companies shouting from the rooftops about how much they care about their customers, and then when we call them to get some help they screw it all up? It's all about delivery. About how focused and tight you are with your work, how simple and clear you are with your communication, and how motivated and dedicated you are with your career.

And this comes from getting down and dirty inside yourself and working your frames until you have that strength: the thinking that gives you the focus, confidence and courage to take that one step forward that you are frightened to take. Delivery comes from moving forward whatever the obstacles are, Out There or in your mind, from contacting people you are scared to contact, from trying new behaviors that you are not used to, and from doing whatever it takes to give the client what she wants. It comes from flexing your strategy, speech and behavior in the face of failure in order to find another route, and then another, until you succeed in achieving what you set out to do. Never giving up.

When you have control of your thinking, both the frames that run the applications and the moment-by-moment thoughts that are the contents of the applications, then your career is guided by a powerful, invisible force that drives you forward in the direction you want to go. This force is so powerful that no matter how hard you try to override it with willpower or forcing your actions, you will always get the results that your force inevitably leads you toward.

That's why it is essential to become aware of your frames and how you approach events during the day in your mind, so that you can take hold of the steering wheel and gain absolute control. If you don't, the force will lead you down paths that may have been OK for you sometime in the distant past, but which today can send you on wild goose chases, wasting your energy and leaving you emotionally exhausted from frustration and disappointment.

If you are working hard and trying to perform at your best and at the same time you are driven by beliefs and conclusions that say things like "Everything comes easier to people with talent," or "It's very easy to lose a client but extremely difficult to win a new one," or "Hard work always pays," then you may be using an operating system that is redundant for you. So many of the common sayings we hear and read every day at work need thinking about very carefully so that we don't allow them to become a part of our own force and mess around with our progress.

Or we may get more personal with frames that say, "I'm not a natural at sales," or "I've never been good with numbers," or "I don't come from the right background," and box ourselves into narrow, tight identities that also put a brake on our progress.

Stop your busyness for a while and quietly look at how you are feeling on a constant basis. What thoughts go through my mind much of the time that make me feel that way? And how does my state contribute to the results I am getting in my career? How do I regularly behave around others? How much value am I actually creating by coming into work every day? And how content am I with where I am and what I am doing? Overall, do I need an operating system update? These are the ways we can wrest back control from the world Out There and put ourselves in pole position on the grid.

Don't waste a moment more struggling, forcing, asserting, and pushing. Take a well-earned break from the outside and turn inwards so that you can set up your own, unique, personal operating system that will enable you to move forward more naturally and more easily. Take back control and get hold of the only real power there is: yourself.

ACKNOWLEDGMENTS

Many thanks to all those who directly and indirectly contributed to me getting to the finish line and publishing my first book. Special thanks to my editor Spencer Borup, my book designer Jason Anscomb, my writing coach Scott Allan, my launch team, and of course to Chandler Bolt and the whole team at Self-Publishing School. I would also like to thank L. Michael Hall, Robert Dilts, Michael Neill, Cal Newport, Louise L. Hay, Dr. Helen Schucman, Chin-Ning Chu, Don Miguel Ruiz, Gabrielle Bernstein, Michael Hyatt, Susan Cain, Seth Godin, Tony Robbins, Joanna Penn, Steven Pressfield, Tim Grahl, and all those who have written books that have led me to where I am today.

ABOUT JAMES IRVINE

James Irvine has had an unusual and varied career as an international banker and a corporate trainer in such places as Germany, The United Arab Emirates, Hong Kong, Brunei and Singapore, where he now lives with his wife Diana. Originally from England, he combines his in-depth understanding of corporate life with a passion for personal development to help people at work take back the control and power that they may have lost along the way. As a Master Practitioner of Neuro-Linguistic Programming, he has learnt that what goes on *inside* of us absolutely controls what happens to us on the *outside*. Today, as an author and speaker, he champions those of us who feel stuck and powerless in their careers and shows them how to regain their self-belief and drive.

If you would like to join the conversation, visit www.irvinejames.com and start on your journey to self-mastery.

www.ingramcontent.com/pod-product-compliance
Lightning Source LLC
Chambersburg PA
CBHW060634210326
41520CB00010B/1595